Isaac Asimov's

21st Century

Library of the Universe

Fact and Fantasy

Is There Life in Outer Space?

BY ISAAC ASIMOV

WITH REVISIONS AND UPDATING BY RICHARD HANTULA

Gareth Stevens Publishing
A WORLD ALMANAC EDUCATION GROUP COMPANY

Please visit our web site at: www.garethstevens.com
For a free color catalog describing Gareth Stevens Publishing's list of high-quality books
and multimedia programs, call 1-800-542-2595 (USA) or 1-800-387-3178 (Canada).
Gareth Stevens Publishing's fax: (414) 332-3567.

Library of Congress Cataloging-in-Publication Data

Asimov, Isaac.
    Is there life in outer space? / by Isaac Asimov; with revisions and updating by Richard Hantula.
        p. cm. — (Isaac Asimov's 21st century library of the universe. Fact and fantasy)
    Includes bibliographical references and index.
    ISBN 0-8368-3950-1 (lib. bdg.)
    1. Life on other planets—Juvenile literature. 2. Cosmology—Juvenile literature.
    I. Hantula, Richard. II. Title.
    QB54.A835   2004
    576.8'39—dc22
                                                    2004048171

This edition first published in 2005 by
Gareth Stevens Publishing
A World Almanac Education Group Company
330 West Olive Street, Suite 100
Milwaukee, WI 53212 USA

Series editor: Betsy Rasmussen
Cover design and layout adaptation: Melissa Valuch
Picture research: Matthew Groshek
Additional picture research: Diane Laska-Swanke
Production director: Jessica Morris
Production assistant: Nicole Esko

The editors at Gareth Stevens Publishing have selected science author Richard Hantula to bring
this classic series of young people's information books up to date. Richard Hantula has written
and edited books and articles on science and technology for more than two decades. He was
the senior U.S. editor for the *Macmillan Encyclopedia of Science*.

In addition to Hantula's contribution to this most recent edition, the editors would like to
acknowledge the participation of two noted science authors, Greg Walz-Chojnacki and
Francis Reddy, as contributors to earlier editions of this work.

Printed in the United States of America

1 2 3 4 5 6 7 8 9 09 08 07 06 05 04

Contents

We live in an enormously large place – the Universe. It's only natural that we would want to understand this place, so scientists and engineers have developed instruments and spacecraft that have told us far more about the Universe than we could possibly imagine.

We have seen planets up close, and spacecraft have even landed on some. We have learned about quasars and pulsars, supernovas and colliding galaxies, and black holes and dark matter. We have gathered amazing data about how the Universe may have come into being and how it may end. Nothing could be more astonishing.

Yet one thing we have not yet discovered is life beyond our Earth. Is it a miraculous accident that only Earthlings may exist in the entire vast Universe? Or has life developed on other worlds?

• Is There Life in Outer Space? •

From Simple Cells

More than three and a half billion years ago, life appeared on our young Earth in the form of tiny cells — perhaps something like the bacteria of today. These simple cells were made of common types of atoms such as carbon, hydrogen, oxygen, nitrogen, and phosphorus.

At first, these atoms made up very simple combinations with each other. But sunlight contains energy, and this energy helped cause the atoms to form more complicated combinations, and cells gradually developed.

On any planet like Earth, with the same chemicals and temperature, many scientists think life might form in the same way. But it is not known how many planets like Earth there may be in the vast Universe.

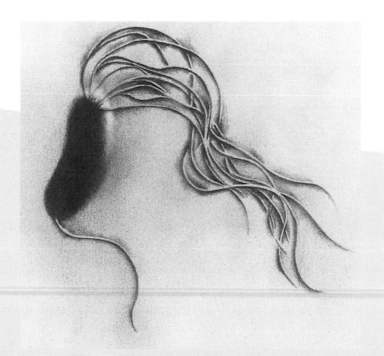

Above: An example of a bacterium. Bacteria, which consist of a single cell, are among the simplest forms of known life.

Above: Our young Earth's deep basins filled with water, forming vast oceans. Large meteorites crashed into the surface. These are the conditions under which life developed on Earth.

Methane + Ethane + Water + Ammonia + Hydrogen Sulfide = Glycine

Above: When all the chemicals pictured are circulated in water and exposed to energy from sunlight, a possible result is the formation of glycine — one of the "building blocks" that help form life.

Most large objects that approach Earth burn up in the atmosphere. But billions of years ago, the atmosphere was different, and comets like this could have delivered their chemicals directly to the surface of our planet.

Life from Space?

The chemicals needed for life probably didn't all exist on Earth when it was very young. Many scientists believe that the necessary chemicals were slowly assembled on our planet as time passed.

But that is not the only possibility. Many of the complex molecules needed for life already existed in space. Astronomers see such chemicals in huge distant clouds between the stars. Such chemicals are also found in comets, on asteroids, and on the moons of some of the planets. Pieces of comets and asteroids are always falling onto Earth — thousands of tons a year. Some scientists think that the chemicals for early life on Earth actually fell from space in such material!

A few researchers even speculate that life may have begun somewhere else in the Universe and may have been carried to Earth — in the form of tiny organisms — by such material! So far, however, there is no proof for this idea.

Left: Billions of tiny grains of comet material like this fall to Earth every day. Many contain the complex chemicals that are the building blocks of life.

Venus — Once Earth's twin?

Venus is almost the same size as Earth and seems to be made up of much the same kinds of rocks as Earth. Venus probably started off with large amounts of water but over time became the hot wasteland that it is today. Venus is closer to the Sun than Earth is, but scientists do not think this is enough to explain the difference between Venus and Earth today. Scientists are not certain why Venus is so different from our planet. Perhaps if they found out, we might be able to prevent Earth from one day becoming like Venus.

A slice through the history of life.on Earth.

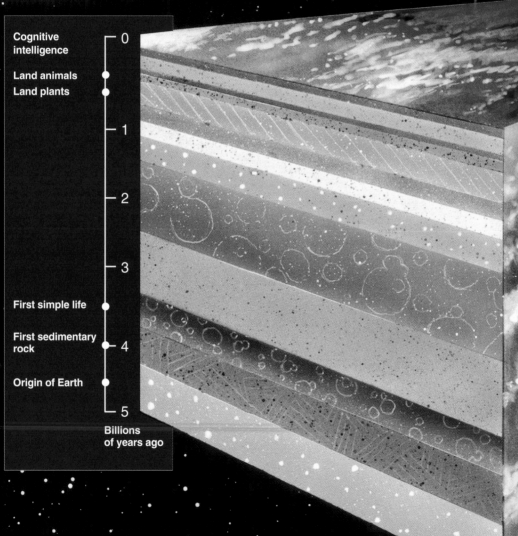

Cognitive
intelligence — 0

Land animals ●
Land plants ●

— 1

— 2

— 3

First simple life ●

First sedimentary
rock — 4

Origin of Earth ●

— 5

Billions
of years ago

Developing Intelligence

For more than a billion years, life on Earth continued to consist of nothing more than simple cells. Gradually, more and more complicated cells developed. These cells eventually − perhaps between one and two billion years ago − started to combine with each other to form larger organisms.

The development of large plants and animals took place within the past 600 million years or so.

Animals that were more complex, and had larger brains, gradually appeared. The slow increase in complexity and in brain size made possible increased intelligence. But it was not until a few million years ago that the ancestors of human beings began the process of developing our present-day human mind and way of thinking. It seems that even though it may be easy for life to develop, it is not so easy for intelligence to develop.

Above: In an experiment, a spark in a mixture of gases common in Earth's early atmosphere causes a brown tar of complex molecules to form.

Above: This diagram shows how simple gases (*upper left square*) and electrical sparks (*upper right square*) could combine to form the complex molecules needed for life on Earth (*bottom squares*).

Above: During the Great Moon Hoax of 1835, the *New York Sun* newspaper reported life on the Moon.

Is There Life on Other Worlds?

For centuries, people have wondered about the possibility of life on other planets. In the 1600s, scientists discovered that the Moon and planets are worlds, just as Earth is a world. Naturally, everyone wondered if there might be life on those worlds, too.

As late as the 1830s, there were articles in a New York newspaper saying that life had been discovered on the Moon. Many people believed what they read, but the story was a hoax. The Moon has almost no atmosphere, and little or no water, and so life as we know it cannot exist there.

In the late nineteenth and early twentieth centuries, certain astronomers thought they saw straight lines on Mars. Some believed these lines were canals that had been built by living beings. But it turned out that even though there may have been much water on Mars at one time, the canals do not exist.

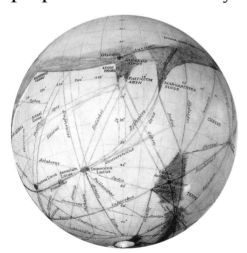

Left: Astronomer Percival Lowell made this globe of Mars in 1901. It shows straight lines that he thought were canals made by Martians.

This is what some people once thought beings on the Moon looked like.

Jupiter — life among the clouds?

The planet Jupiter consists mainly of hydrogen and helium, largely in the form of gas. Other substances — like ammonia, methane, water, and carbon — are present in small amounts. The planet's atmosphere is huge. Its outer layers are very frigid. Farther down, it gets very hot, with temperatures of thousands of degrees. Temperatures are comfortable at intermediate layers. Could life-forms exist at the intermediate level of Jupiter's atmosphere?

11

Above: The barren Martian landscape, in a 2004 view from the rover vehicle *Spirit*. Scientists enhanced the colors to bring out the different kinds of rocks and soil in the area.

Mars — once a living planet?

Probes that landed on Mars in the 1970s and 1990s found no life as we know it, and all the water on the planet was frozen. Still, there are markings on the planet's surface that look like dry riverbeds and seabeds. New probes that explored the Martian surface in 2004 revealed more evidence of abundant water in the planet's past. Is it possible that Mars was once warmer than it is now? If so, it may once have been home to life. Even now, simple life-forms may exist there that the probes did not detect.

Zeroing In on Other Worlds

Until a few decades ago, scientists could observe other worlds in the Solar System only from a great distance. Only from very far away could they gather data, on the basis of which they concluded that these worlds were too cold, too hot, too dry, or too hostile for life as we know it to develop. But then it became possible to send probes into space to photograph and closely study conditions on other worlds in the Solar System. Probes have been sent to the Moon since the late 1950s, and to planets since the early 1960s.

Humans have even landed on the Moon, and probes have landed on Mars and Venus. These probes have shown Venus to be boiling hot. They have also shown that Mars has no canals and its surface today seems to be mostly waterless. As of early 2004, no signs of even the simplest life had turned up on any of these worlds.

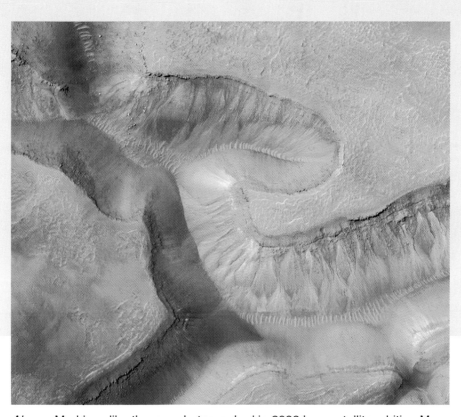

Above: Markings like these – photographed in 2000 by a satellite orbiting Mars – suggest that water may have flowed on the Red Planet's surface long ago.

COSMIC QUEST

8 Your tests show hole in Earth's ozone layer may be getting bigger. Risks to life on Earth could become high. Urgent that you report your findings in person. Return to home base on Earth.

34 Was Mars a living planet? Read about it in the Mystery Box on page 12, and sit out your next turn.

39 Pick up meteoroid samples from asteroid belt to examine for signs of chemical "building blocks" of life. Wait out next turn.

30 NASA and European Space Agency missions to Mars yield great advances in our understanding of the Red Planet. Advance three spaces.

15 Navigator believes intelligent-life-on-Moon hoax and wants to make an unscheduled lunar landing. Return to Earth to pick up a new navigator.

52 Submarine probe explores Jupiter's moon Europa in search of an oasis of life beneath the icy surface. Advance two spaces.

18 *Mariner 10* has mapped out nearly half of Mercury's surface. Your ship's probe must map the rest. Sit out next turn.

27 Your probe maps Venus through its clouds. Stay there to study results. Sit out your next turn.

44 Could there be life among Jupiter's clouds? Explore the possibilities by reading the Mystery Box on page 11 – and advance two spaces!

56 Ship sends probe into hazy atmosphere of Saturn's largest moon, Titan. Wait out next turn as probe collects samples.

21 Advance probe drifting too close to Sun. Go back one space to repair damaged craft.

24 Could Venus and Earth once have been mistaken for twins? Sit out your next turn while you read the Mystery Box on page 7.

47 Lightning poses a great hazard to your landing party's descent into Jupiter's atmosphere. Drop back two spaces.

64 Uranus probe crashes against huge cliffs of Miranda, Uranus's craggy moon. Drop back one space.

Cosmic Quest Game

So much more is known about the Solar System now than just a few years ago. We have mapped Venus through its clouds, and we know that its surface is hot enough to melt lead. It has an atmosphere that is more than ninety times thicker than Earth's and is made up mostly of carbon dioxide. The clouds on Venus contain deadly sulfuric acid.

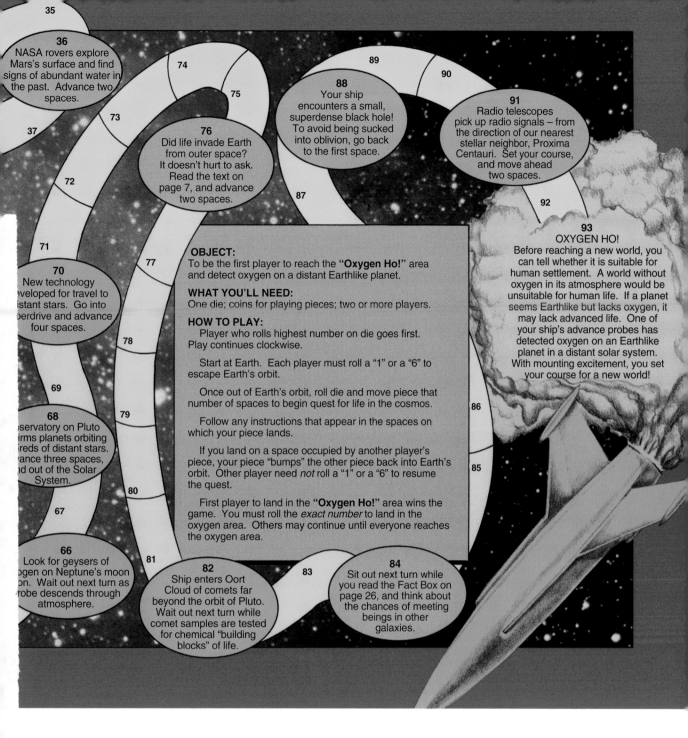

35

36
NASA rovers explore Mars's surface and find signs of abundant water in the past. Advance two spaces.

37

73

74

75

72

76
Did life invade Earth from outer space? It doesn't hurt to ask. Read the text on page 7, and advance two spaces.

71

77

70
New technology developed for travel to distant stars. Go into overdrive and advance four spaces.

78

69

79

68
Observatory on Pluto confirms planets orbiting hundreds of distant stars. Advance three spaces, and out of the Solar System.

80

67

66
Look for geysers of oxygen on Neptune's moon Triton. Wait out next turn as probe descends through atmosphere.

81

82
Ship enters Oort Cloud of comets far beyond the orbit of Pluto. Wait out next turn while comet samples are tested for chemical "building blocks" of life.

83

84
Sit out next turn while you read the Fact Box on page 26, and think about the chances of meeting beings in other galaxies.

89

90

88
Your ship encounters a small, superdense black hole! To avoid being sucked into oblivion, go back to the first space.

87

91
Radio telescopes pick up radio signals – from the direction of our nearest stellar neighbor, Proxima Centauri. Set your course, and move ahead two spaces.

92

93
OXYGEN HO!
Before reaching a new world, you can tell whether it is suitable for human settlement. A world without oxygen in its atmosphere would be unsuitable for human life. If a planet seems Earthlike but lacks oxygen, it may lack advanced life. One of your ship's advance probes has detected oxygen on an Earthlike planet in a distant solar system. With mounting excitement, you set your course for a new world!

86

85

OBJECT:
To be the first player to reach the **"Oxygen Ho!"** area and detect oxygen on a distant Earthlike planet.

WHAT YOU'LL NEED:
One die; coins for playing pieces; two or more players.

HOW TO PLAY:
Player who rolls highest number on die goes first. Play continues clockwise.

Start at Earth. Each player must roll a "1" or a "6" to escape Earth's orbit.

Once out of Earth's orbit, roll die and move piece that number of spaces to begin quest for life in the cosmos.

Follow any instructions that appear in the spaces on which your piece lands.

If you land on a space occupied by another player's piece, your piece "bumps" the other piece back into Earth's orbit. Other player need *not* roll a "1" or a "6" to resume the quest.

First player to land in the **"Oxygen Ho!"** area wins the game. You must roll the *exact number* to land in the oxygen area. Others may continue until everyone reaches the oxygen area.

Mars, meanwhile, has a thin atmosphere, only about 1/100 as thick as Earth's, and its surface is often colder than Antarctica. Jupiter is a huge ball consisting largely of hydrogen, helium, and other gases, and so are the other large planets – Saturn, Uranus, and Neptune. Their moons seem to be lumps of rock and ice. These facts indicate that Earth is the only known planet that can support life like ours.

An artist imagines life existing in an ocean under the icy surface of Europa, one of Jupiter's moons.

Possibilities of Other Life

Although the worlds of our Solar System beyond Mars cannot support life like ours, might some of them have other forms of life?

Even on Earth, life exists in places where conditions are much harsher than what we are used to. For example, microorganisms have been found living in oil deposits lying below Earth's surface, in boiling water rising from springs (or "hydrothermal vents") on the ocean floor, and in Antarctica.

One of Jupiter's satellites, Europa, seems to be covered with a crust of ice. Perhaps an ocean lies under the ice. Might it contain life-forms like those living in harsh conditions on Earth or even completely different from anything on Earth?

One of Saturn's satellites, Titan, has a thick atmosphere. Under this atmosphere, there may be water and other chemicals that might support life. Could there be some type of life there, too?

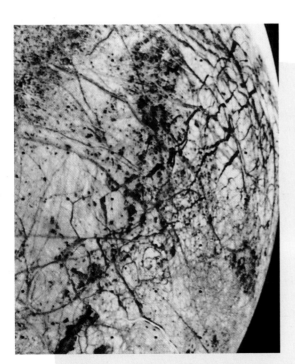

Above: Europa, under whose icy surface there may lie a vast ocean.

Above: On Earth, in addition to tiny microorganisms, strange creatures like these tube worms are found in places on the ocean bottom where deep-sea volcanoes vent.

Billions of Opportunities

Scientists are fairly certain there is no life like ours anywhere in our Solar System besides Earth. But there are other stars in our Milky Way Galaxy and beyond, and at least some of them have planets circling them.

Our Galaxy may have as many as 400 billion stars, and there are more than 100 billion other galaxies. Even if only one percent of the stars is like our Sun, and only one percent of those stars has planets like Earth, that would still mean there could be billions of Earthlike planets. Perhaps life exists on every one of them. Perhaps on a few of them, civilizations may have developed. Some of these civilizations might even be advanced far beyond our own. At this time, scientists have no way of telling.

We live on one of nine known planets orbiting our Sun (*below*) — one of as many as 400 billion stars in the Milky Way Galaxy (*left, inset*), which is one of billions of galaxies (*left*) in the Universe.

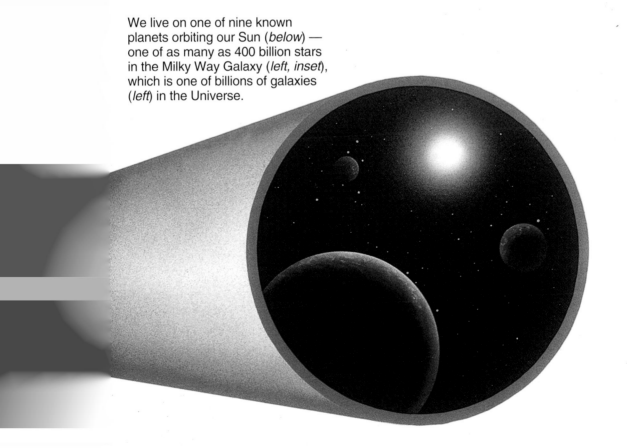

Above: These radio telescope antennas at the Hat Creek Observatory in northern California search for alien signals from the stars. Scientists expect to have 350 of the radio "dishes" at the site by 2005.

The Search for Extraterrestrial Intelligence

If there are billions of "Earths" in the Universe, how can we find them?

Many scientists are convinced that we can detect radio signals from extraterrestrials. The first radio telescopes were built to study the radio waves from stars and galaxies. Now radio telescopes are also being used as "big ears" to try to detect signals that may be coming from intelligent beings on another world. In addition to looking for such radio pulses, scientists have started using telescopes to search for light signals from aliens. These signals might be flashes or other forms of light that do not match naturally occurring patterns.

This hunt for signs of intelligent life on other worlds is known as the Search for Extraterrestrial Intelligence, or SETI. The work is sponsored by organizations of scientists and other interested persons such as the SETI Institute, the SETI League, and the Planetary Society. Anyone with a computer and access to the Internet can take part in the SETI effort by running the freely available SETI@home program on their computer. This program helps process the massive amounts of data that are produced by the search.

I Love Lucy is out of this world

We know of one civilization that has been sending radio signals into space — us! For decades, radio broadcasts have been heading out into the Universe from Earth. They have unique patterns that aliens could recognize as intelligent. So far, radio signals, which travel at the speed of light, have journeyed several dozen light-years from our home. TV broadcasts, which are also radio waves, have traveled more than fifty light-years. Who knows, maybe some aliens are watching *I Love Lucy*!

All Shapes and Sizes

Even here on Earth, life takes a wide variety of shapes.

Compare a whale and a sardine. Then compare a whale with a crow. Compare a praying mantis and a lady bug. Then compare a praying mantis with a horse. Compare a bacterium and an oak tree. Then compare the oak tree with a giant redwood.

On other worlds, life probably would develop in certain ways to fit certain environments. Some of the life-forms might seem unpleasant to us, and some beautiful, just like here on Earth.

Perhaps, in studying completely different life-forms, we will better understand all of life — and ourselves.

Above: Lake Hoare on the continent of Antarctica. Scientists are studying Antarctic lakes to learn more about past environments on Mars.

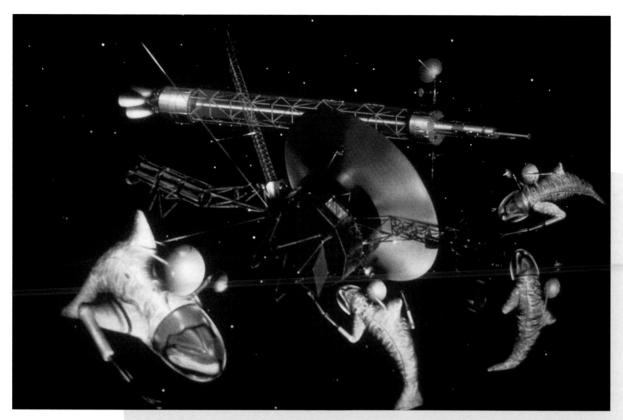

Above: An artist imagines dolphinlike life-forms making contact with a *Voyager* probe far beyond our Solar System.

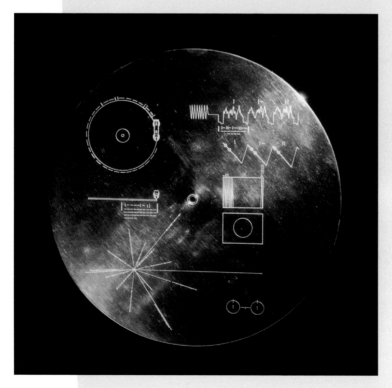

Left: The *Voyager 1* and *Voyager 2* space probes carry photographs of Earth and a phonograph recording of music and human voices. The record jacket (shown) explains how to play the record and where all the items originated.

Worlds Away

Suppose there is life on planets orbiting other stars. Can you imagine traveling to those planets to study other life-forms? Rockets that can reach the Moon in just a few days and Mars in a few months would take many years to reach the stars.

Future spaceships might go as fast as 40,000 miles (64,000 kilometers) a second, but it would still take more than twenty years to reach the nearest star. Even if you traveled at the speed of light (the fastest possible speed), it would take 100,000 years to go from one end of our Galaxy to the other.

If there is advanced life among the stars, how will we reach it? Or will we Earthlings remain alone?

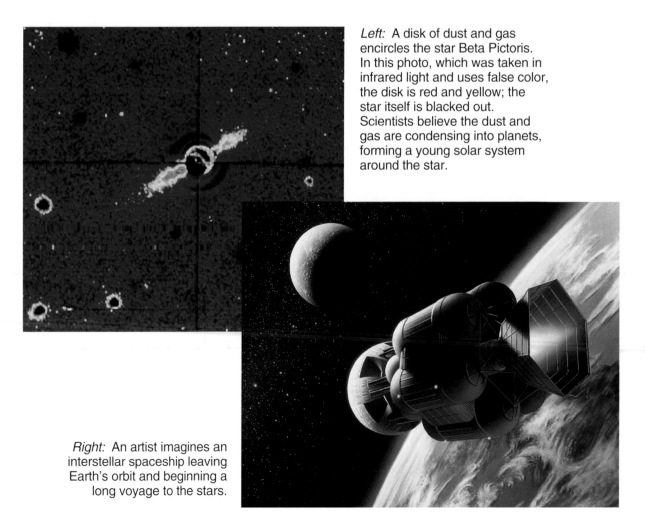

Left: A disk of dust and gas encircles the star Beta Pictoris. In this photo, which was taken in infrared light and uses false color, the disk is red and yellow; the star itself is blacked out. Scientists believe the dust and gas are condensing into planets, forming a young solar system around the star.

Right: An artist imagines an interstellar spaceship leaving Earth's orbit and beginning a long voyage to the stars.

In this illustration, the spaceship from Earth nears its new home – the planetary system of a remote star.

25

Could We Be Aliens?

Reaching the stars will take time. Imagine starships that are small worlds in themselves, with 100,000 people aboard each one. Imagine these ships traveling through space on voyages that last thousands of years. One ship might eventually reach a distant planet, and the other ships might continue on to other worlds.

Slowly, human beings would settle among the stars and perhaps encounter other forms of life. Because of the great distances and time involved, it would be difficult for one settlement to communicate with another. Therefore, each might develop in isolation. After a while, Earth might become just a distant memory.

Our descendants might become aliens to other interstellar civilizations.

Left: An artist's conception of an alien who has come to Earth from space.

The distant galaxies — plenty to go around

There might be enough suitable planets in our Galaxy for millions of settlements. Beyond our Galaxy, there are billions more galaxies. Right "nearby" are a few small ones: the Large Magellanic Cloud (roughly 160,000 light-years away), the Small Magellanic Cloud (about 200,000 light-years away), and a couple of closer dwarf galaxies. The nearest large galaxy is the Andromeda Galaxy. It is larger than our own Galaxy and is about 2.2 million light-years away. The farthest known galaxies may be more than 13 billion light-years away.

After centuries of travel, an Earth ship and its inhabitants prepare for arrival on a new world.

Fact File: Hidden Life

If we do not find any life-forms in a specific place, such as a distant planet or even a house in the neighborhood, we might call that place "uninhabited." But actually, an "uninhabited" house is filled with many life-forms — even if we don't see any of them at first glance. Many of these life-forms seem alien to us, and they live under conditions that might seem hostile for life to survive. The photographs shown here describe just a few of these life-forms.

2. Some **bacteria** have tough shells that protect them against hostile surroundings.

2

1

KEY TO THE "UNINHABITED HOUSE"

1. Some life-forms need surroundings that would kill other life-forms, including humans. For example, this **bacterium** needs an environment *without* air!

8

Could it be that, like our "uninhabited" house, other planets harbor unusual life-forms surviving under harsh conditions — and that we just haven't found them yet?

8. **Fleas** don't need a dog in order to live. They do quite well amid hair, droppings, and dirty rugs and bedding.

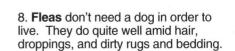

28

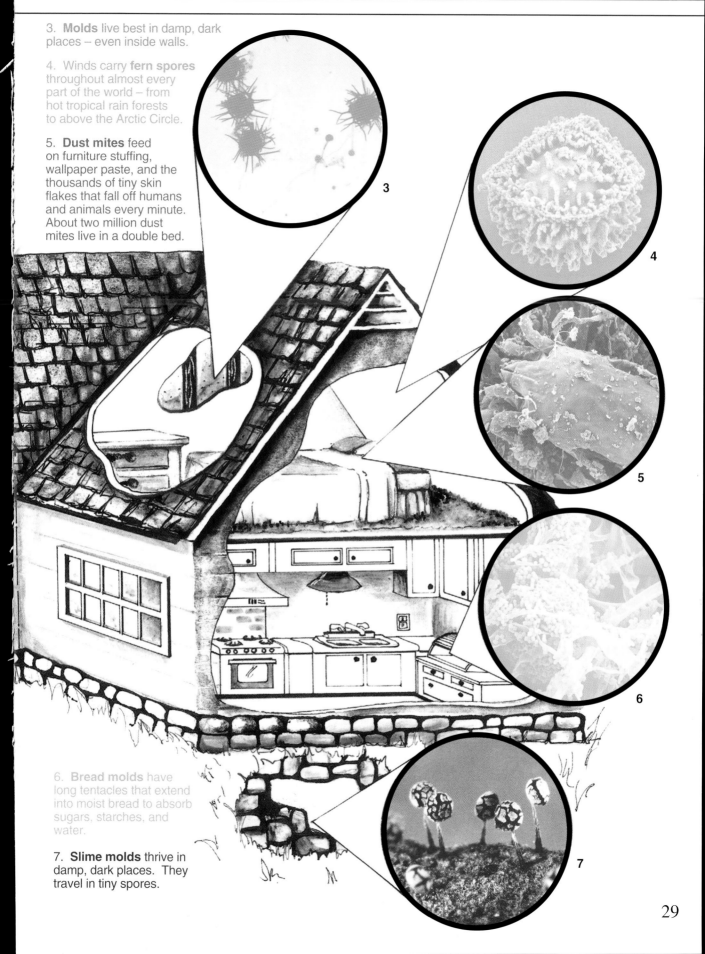

3. **Molds** live best in damp, dark places – even inside walls.

4. Winds carry **fern spores** throughout almost every part of the world – from hot tropical rain forests to above the Arctic Circle.

5. **Dust mites** feed on furniture stuffing, wallpaper paste, and the thousands of tiny skin flakes that fall off humans and animals every minute. About two million dust mites live in a double bed.

6. **Bread molds** have long tentacles that extend into moist bread to absorb sugars, starches, and water.

7. **Slime molds** thrive in damp, dark places. They travel in tiny spores.

3

4

5

6

7

29

More Books about Life in Outer Space

Astronomy Encyclopedia. Patrick Moore and Leif Robinson (Oxford)
Cosmic Company: The Search for Life in the Universe. Seth Shostak and Alex Barnett
   (Cambridge)
Encyclopedia of Space Exploration. Joseph A. Angelo Jr. (Facts on File)
Extraterrestrials: A Field Guide for Earthlings. Terence Dickinson and Adolf Schaller
   (Camden House)
Life in Outer Space: The Search for Extraterrestrials. Kim McDonald (Raintree Steck-Vaughn)
Looking for Life in the Universe: The Search for Extraterrestrial Intelligence. Ellen Jackson
   (Houghton Mifflin)
Space Aliens. Steve Parker (Raintree Steck-Vaughn)
UFOs. Jacqueline Laks Gorman (Gareth Stevens)

DVDs

The Standard Deviants: Astronomy Adventure. (Cerebellum)

UFOs & Aliens. (Questar)

Web Sites

The Internet sites listed here can help you learn more about planets outside our Solar System
and about possible life in the Universe beyond Earth.

Planetary Society. www.planetary.org/html/UPDATES/seti/
PlanetQuest: The Search for Another Earth. planetquest.jpl.nasa.gov/
SETI@home. setiathome.ssl.berkeley.edu/
SETI Institute. www.seti-inst.edu/
SETI League. www.setileague.org/
Space.com: Search for Extraterrestrial Life and SETI. www.space.com/searchforlife/
Students for the Exploration and Development of Space (SEDS). www.seds.org/

Places to Visit

Here are some museums and centers where you can explore the Universe and the
possibility of life beyond our Earth.

**Adler Planetarium and
 Astronomy Museum**
1300 S. Lake Shore Drive
Chicago, Illinois 60605

American Museum of Natural History
Rose Center for Earth and Space
Central Park West at 79th Street
New York, NY 10024

**International UFO Museum and
 Research Center**
114 North Main Street
Roswell, New Mexico 88203

National Air and Space Museum
Smithsonian Institution
6th and Independence Avenue SW
Washington, DC 20560

Odyssium
11211 142nd Street
Edmonton, Alberta T5M4A1
Canada

Scienceworks Museum
2 Booker Street
Spotswood, Victoria 3015
Australia

Glossary

atmosphere: the gases that surround a planet, star, or moon.

atoms: the smallest particles that can exist of the basic substances called elements.

bacteria: a group of small, simple life-forms that consist of a single cell. A single one of them is said to be a bacterium. Bacteria are found in a great many places, such as soil, water, air, food, plants, and animals, including humans.

black hole: an object in space whose gravity is so strong that not even light can escape from inside it. A black hole is thought to result when a very large star explodes and collapses.

carbon dioxide: a heavy, colorless, odorless gas. On Earth, it is exhaled by humans and animals and absorbed by plants.

European Space Agency: an organization for space research and exploration sponsored by several European countries.

extraterrestrial: "outside of Earth." *Extraterrestrial* refers to forms of life that do not begin on Earth.

galaxy: a large star system containing up to hundreds of billions of stars, along with gas and dust.

hoax: an act that is intended to deceive.

hydrogen: the lightest gas in Earth's atmosphere. It is the most common gas in the atmospheres of the large outer planets of the Solar System.

interstellar: between or among the stars.

light-year: the distance that light travels in one year — nearly six trillion miles (9.6 trillion km).

methane: an odorless, colorless, flammable gas. It is an important source of hydrogen. It was one of the gases present in the early atmosphere of Earth.

microorganism: an organism that is so small it can be seen only through a microscope.

Milky Way: the glowing mist of stars in the sky that is our Galaxy.

NASA: the National Aeronautics and Space Administration — the government space agency in the United States.

organism: anything that lives, such as a bacterium, a plant, or an animal.

oxygen: the gas in Earth's atmosphere that makes human and animal life possible.

probe: a craft that travels in space, photographing and studying celestial bodies and in some cases even landing on them.

radio waves: electromagnetic waves that can be detected by radio-receiving equipment.

satellite: a small body that circles, or orbits, around a larger body. The Moon is Earth's natural satellite.

SETI: The Search for Extraterrestrial Intelligence — various programs that look for signs of extraterrestrial intelligence by trying to detect radio or light signals that such intelligence might use.

Solar System: the Sun with the planets and all the other bodies, such as asteroids, that orbit it.

spore: a small body — usually consisting of a single cell — from which a new organism can grow.

sulfuric acid: a liquid that is capable of burning, wearing away, or dissolving many materials.

Voyager 1 and 2: two U.S. space probes that were launched in 1977 and are heading out into interstellar space.

Index

Born in 1920, Isaac Asimov came to the United States as a young boy from his native Russia. As a young man, he was a student of biochemistry. In time, he became one of the most productive writers the world has ever known. His books cover a spectrum of topics, including science, history, language theory, fantasy, and science fiction. His brilliant imagination gained him the respect and admiration of adults and children alike. Sadly, Isaac Asimov died shortly after the publication of the first edition of *Isaac Asimov's Library of the Universe.*

The publishers wish to thank the following for permission to reproduce copyright material: front cover, 3, © Mark Newman/Visuals Unlimited; 4, 5 (lower), Matthew Groshek/© Gareth Stevens, Inc.; 5 (upper), © Dorothy Sigler Norton; 6, © Shigemi Numazawa; 7, 13, 22, NASA; 8, 9 (right), © Garret Moore 1988; 9 (left), Courtesy of Dr. Bishun Khare/Cornell University; 10, Don Davis/Courtesy of Sky Publishing Corporation; 11 (left), Courtesy of Lowell Observatory; 11 (right), © Lee Bataglia; 12, NASA/JPL/Cornell; 14-15, Kate Kriege/© Gareth Stevens, Inc.; 16, © Sally Bensusen 1988; 17 (left), 23 (lower), 24 (left), Jet Propulsion Laboratory; 17 (right), © Dudley Foster, Woods Hole Oceanographic Institution; 18-19, © Julian Baum 1988; 20, Dr. James R. Forster, Hat Creek, California; 23 (upper), © Rick Sternbach; 24 (right), 25, © Doug McLeod 1988; 26, © Andrew C. Stewart/Fortean Picture Library; 27, © George Peirson 1988; 28 (upper left), © Theresa Fassel 1988; 28 (upper right), © J. Coggins 1988; 28 (lower), 29 (lower center right), © Marilyn Schaller 1988; 28-29 (house), Gérard Franquin/© Père Castor Flammarion; 29 (upper left), 29 (lower), © Runk/Schoenberger from Grant Heilman; 29 (upper right), © Betsy Esselman; 29 (upper center right), Science Photo Library.